Kingdom Kids Collection

START NOW

THE WORKBOOK

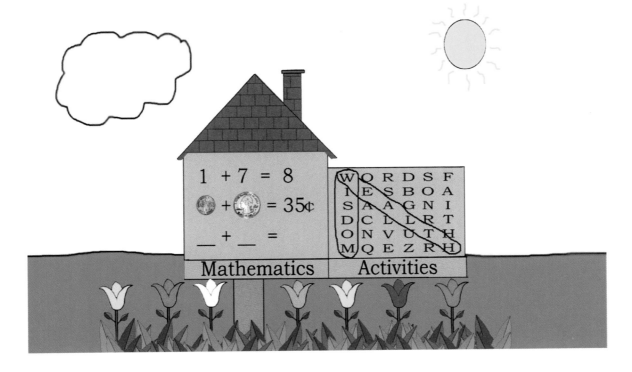

Illustrated by Elisha Bradley

Rosalin L. Terry

Limits of Liability and Disclaimer of Warranty

The author and publisher shall not be liable for your misuse of this material. This book is strictly for informational and educational purposes. The purpose of this book is to educate and entertain. The author and/or publisher do not guarantee that anyone following these techniques, suggestions, tips, ideas, or strategies will become successful. The author and/or publisher shall have neither liability nor responsibility to anyone with respect to any loss or damage caused, or alleged to be caused, directly or indirectly by the information contained in this book.

Views expressed in this publication do not necessarily reflect the views of the publisher.

Printed in the United States of America

ISBN 978-1-948270-08-3

START NOW: The Kingdom Kids Collection Series of books are designed to inspire and simply educate children regarding the principles of money. This series was written to encourage families to introduce the concepts and principles of money and wealth to their children at an early age. It is very important for families to teach children about money. We use money to achieve and acquire many things. Without it, our survival can be difficult.

Mostly everything has a price tag attached to it. This series is a great way for the entire family to learn about money. As children learn more about money, they will become excited about learning to save it for the things they desire. Teaching children these concepts at an early age will allow them to make smart financial decisions once they become adults.

The purpose of this series is to encourage families to push their children toward a path of being debt free. This series is simple enough to be read to toddlers, yet informative enough for the entire family. The books are not just to be read, but they also include practical examples and exercises that can be applied by the entire family. Don't wait to start teaching your children about money! START NOW by exercising your faith and building a life of fit finances for the generations to come!

START NOW: The Workbook is designed to accompany the START NOW four-part Kingdom Kids Collection series. The Workbook includes various exercises and activities to inspire, test, and sharpen the skills and mindset of the children who have read the series. Children will enhance their mathematical training and reading comprehension, awaken their creativity, and develop fresh and exciting ideas that will prepare them for success and financial freedom. The Workbook also aims to develop values such as integrity, continuous learning, resiliency, and responsibility. Thanks for taking the time to START NOW!

These principals also teach them to tap into their purpose and destiny, to be disciplined in spending/saving habits, math calculations, to invest in their future, and to wisely build and maintain wealth as well as financial freedom. These books are catered to Ages 0 to 12 and give fun examples and creative ideas on ways to execute the principles. START NOW!!!

Abundant Blessings,

Rosalin L. Terry

"I can do all things through Christ who strengthens me."

Philippians 4:13 NKJV

Contents

Introduction

START NOW: The Workbook is designed to help your children put to practice the skills, principles, and knowledge learned in the Start Now series. You can use it along with the other books or you can use it after completing the series. The Workbook contains activities that connect with Common Core Standards for Pre-K, 1st Grade, 2nd Grade, 3rd Grade and 4th Grade. They include skills such as Fine and Gross Motor Skills, Color Recognition, Coin Recognition, Counting to Ten, Collecting Data, Determining Coin Value, Addition, and Vocabulary Knowledge. Standards may differ per state. Additionally, the activities within this workbook provide opportunities for children to think outside of the box and tap into their creativity. More than anything, START NOW: The Workbook is a great way for families to come together and discuss money in a way that is fun and informative for the entire family. With so many different activities, there's something in the Start Now Workbook for everyone to enjoy!

SAVING COINS

Color the piggy banks.

pink

purple

yellow

green

blue

orange

red

Any color

Draw a line to match each coin with its name.

PENNY

NICKEL

DIME

QUARTER

18

COUNTING COINS

Write the number of coins.

Write the value of each set of coins.

_____

_____

_____

LEARNING MONEY PRINCIPLES

Find your way through the maze to get the pot of gold coins. Start at the bottom left opening. START NOW!

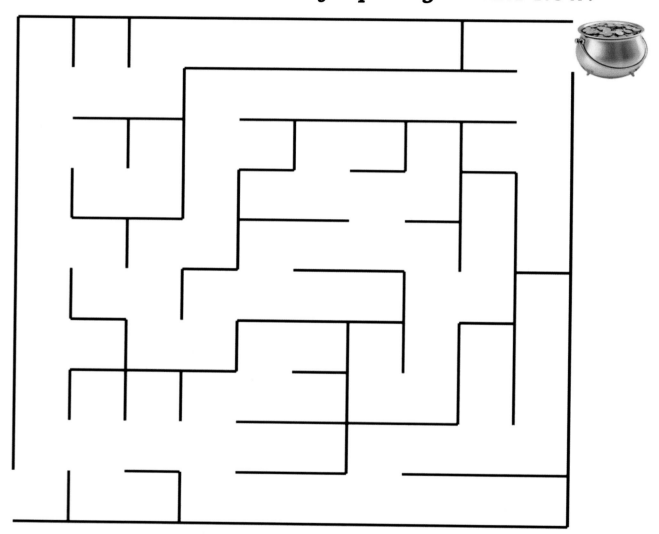

FIND YOUR PASSION

Discover something that you like to do as a service to others or as a creator of a good. It may be baking, making things, or repairing items. It could also be providing a service to others. Whatever you decide to do, the challenge is to create and run your own business for 30 days. Be as unique as you desire. Collect five piggy banks, envelopes, jars, etc. Label each with a principle below. Each time you earn money, apply the five Money Principles below and divide the income. There is a percentage listed beside each principle. Write down your results. After you have completed your challenge, share your results with a friend or family member and challenge them to join you. Feel free to keep it going. START NOW!

1. Tithe (10%) _____

2. Give (10%) _____

3. Save (10%) _____

4. Invest (20%) _____

5. Spend (50%) _____

SAVINGS CHALLENGE

Below you will find a chart that lists various dollar amounts. You are challenged to color each box as you save that particular amount. Place the money in your savings piggy bank or container. Once you have completed the challenge, you will have saved **$250**. After the challenge is complete, have your parents open a Savings Account for you at a local bank. START NOW!

START NOW				
SAVINGS CHART				
$10	$20	$5	$1	$7
$12	$5	$8	$3	$9
$4	$15	$25	$16	$22
$2	$11	$8	$16	$10
$7	$4	$9	$12	$8

STRATEGIES TO BUILD WEALTH

List four strategies that can be used to acquire wealth.

1. _____

2. _____

3. _____

4. _____

Complete the word puzzle.

```
S C D G H M O N E Y E B P Q E O A X
A P H M K N S N N G T S E V N I Q B
V C E S G I V E O G Y E P J E O R P
E C M N H M C N T Y E E P G E Z S S
S C O G D M P R I N C I P L E S U E
B C C G H I C N T Y Z E P G E R R S
S A N J H M N N E P Y E P Q E M J N
B C I G F M C G O S E C N A N I F I
A E B G H M M D T I T H E N G E O O
J E W E L R Y E T Y B U D G E T V C
```

Budget	Spending	Income	Principles	Jewelry	Finances
Coins	Give	Tithe	Invest	Money	Savings

CHARACTER BUILDING CHALLENGES

Challenge 1

Write six positive character traits to describe yourself in the flower petals below. Read them daily and remind yourself how awesome and brilliant you really are! START NOW!

Challenge 2

As we build wealth, we must also grow in our level of gratitude. Below, you are challenged to make a collage of people, things, and ideas that you are grateful to know or have. If the space below is too small, feel free to get a poster board, dry erase board, or a sheet of construction paper. Be creative! Use markers, paint, magazines, photos, etc. to bring life to your collage. START NOW!

I AM THANKFUL FOR...

44

Challenge 3

Let's work on building fortitude. Below you are challenged to write at least ten statements or quotes that you may use throughout life to help you stay encouraged and strengthened when things appear to be negative or out of your control. Ask your parent or guardian, teacher, or another positive family member to help you. Take the time to meditate on these statements daily. When you are faced with a challenge or conflict, reflect on the statements you write below. START NOW!

1.	6.
2.	7.
3.	8.
4.	9.
5.	10.

VOCABULARY

Define the following vocabulary words.

1. Advertise
2. Allowance
3. Barter
4. Budget
5. Expense
6. Generate

7. Goods
8. Income
9. Kingdom
10. Pray
11. Purpose
12. Service
13. Vision
14. Wealth

About the Author

Rosalin L. Terry has a very diverse professional background as she has studied Accounting, Business Management, Massage Therapy, and Fashion Design & Merchandising all of which she obtained a college degree. She enjoys financial planning, budgeting, and sharing wisdom & knowledge with others. Her passion is for every child and family unit to know the principles of money and to live a life that affords him/her the opportunity to build and maintain wealth while enjoying financial freedom.

About the Illustrator

Elisha Bradley is a native of Tennessee and known as an illustrator, graphic designer, and digital artist. He is the owner of E-Studios and comes from a background of artist and musicians, which consist of his talented siblings. Elisha also does freelance art and music in Murfreesboro, TN and the surrounding Nashville, TN area and occasionally within other states. Elisha's style of art is broad with ranges from abstract images to cartoon/comic characters, with strengths in realism and surrealism. He believes that attention to detail is key and therefore favors realism. Elisha hopes to convey to the audience a message by which they can see and feel the emotions and body language through character images as he illustrates them.

ALSO BY ROSALIN L. TERRY

 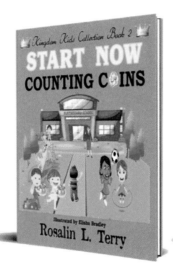  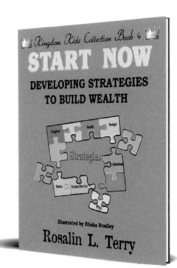

STAY CONNECTED

Thank you for purchasing START NOW: The Workbook. Rosalin would like to connect with you! Below are a few ways you can connect with Rosalin.

instagram rosinspired

facebook Rosalin Terry/ Ros Inspired

twitter rosinspired

website www.rosinspired.com

Made in the USA
Middletown, DE
04 January 2020

82394781R00029